Where
My Wellies
Take Me ...

Designed & illustrated by
OLIVIA LOMENECH GILL

A TEMPLAR BOOK

First published in the UK in 2012 by Templar Publishing,
an imprint of The Templar Company Limited,
The Granary, North Street, Dorking, Surrey,
RH4 1DN, UK
www.templarco.co.uk

Text copyright © 2012 by Michael Morpurgo
Illustration copyright © 2012 by Olivia Lomenech Gill

First edition

ISBN 978-1-84877-544-2

Edited by Jane Feaver

Printed in China

templar publishing
www.templarco.co.uk

CLARE AND MICHAEL
MORPURGO

Where
My Wellies
Take Me ...

To our family – Clare and Michael

To Gabhran and Elzéard – Olivia

CLARE & MICHAEL MORPURGO

When you're older your mind goes back often to the best (yes, and to the worst) times of your childhood. For Clare and for me, some of the happiest years of our lives were spent growing up in the countryside. I used to wander the marshes and sea walls near my childhood home in Bradwell on the Essex coast, the haunt of hares and lapwings, of foxes and herons. Meanwhile Clare (unknown to me then) was out in her wellies, tramping the deep lanes of Devon around the village of Iddesleigh, riding the farmers' horses, searching the graveyard for lizards and slow-worms, collecting birds' skulls and shells and stripy stones from the river. We had walked on the wild side, gone where our wellies had taken us, and loved it.

Later on – much later on – both of us teachers by now, we came up with an idea that we hoped would enable as many children as possible to do exactly what we had done: to walk up windswept hillsides, to stomp through snow, squelch through muddy gateways, save tadpoles from shrinking puddles, and watch salmon rising in the river. Along with friends, we set up a charity and called it Farms for City Children. In the last thirty years or more, over 100,000 city children have spent a week of their lives on the three farms – Nethercott, here in Devon where it all began; Treginnis in Wales, on the spectacular coast outside St Davids; and Wick Court by the River Severn in Gloucestershire. The children become farmers for a week –

they feed the sheep and calves, muck out the horses, dig up potatoes. They wear wellies almost all the time, and in among their tasks they have the freedom to explore and enjoy the countryside around them, just as we did.

Clare is in her seventieth year now and I'm catching up fast. What better way to celebrate, we thought, than to make a book together for the first time. So I, with a little help from Clare, would write a story about a young girl walking the lanes of Devon and she, with a little bit of help from me, would choose some of her favourite poems. Both of us had a lot of help from our good friend Jane Feaver, who lives down the lane. And we found by the greatest good fortune a wonderful artist, Olivia Lomenech Gill, who has conceived the book as it now looks, produced the wonderful paintings and drawings, and written it all out, just as Pippa would have done, by hand.

Every copy of the book that is sold will help support more children to come down to our farms. So, even if you didn't know it at the time, thank you for buying this. Now we hope you enjoy reading it as much as we have loved putting it all together.

Clare and Michael Morpurgo

February 2012

A List of Poems in This Book

"Where are you off to, Pippa?"

It's what Aunty Peggy always asks me when I'm on my way out.

"Wherever," I tell her, with a shrug. "Where my wellies take me."

"Pippa!" she says, giving me a look. She thinks I'm trying to be funny, or a bit too 'poetic'. I'm not. Anyway, it's her fault I like poetry so much. Every night before bed, she reads me one of her favourite poems.

The other thing I love about staying with Aunty Peggy is going for walks. I never have any idea of where I'm going, I just go. ~~Prop~~ Proper, long walks. I don't care if it's raining, don't care if it's cold.

But it's sunshiny this morning, sitting on the front step in the sun, pulling on my wellies.

"Four o'clock, Pippa," Aunty Peggy calls after me. "Don't forget it's May Day. It all begins at four. Don't be late, dear. You don't want to miss the fun, do you?"

I'm not mad about games and I hate races, so yes, I want to miss the whole horrible thing if I can. But I know enough not to say it out loud. My wellies are off on a walk, and I'm going with them. So I just give her a wave ...

Me putting on my WELLIES!

11

and I'm off !

① BLACKBIRD

1   2   3

TEWKESBURY ROAD

It is good to be out on the road,
  and going one knows not where,
Going through meadow and village,
  one knows not whither or why;
Through the grey light drift of the dust,
  in the keen cool rush of the air,
Under the flying white clouds,
  and the broad blue lift of the sky.

And to halt at the chattering brook,
  in a tall green fern at the brink
Where the harebell grows, and the gorse,
  and the foxgloves purple and white;
Where the shy-eyed delicate deer
  troop down to the brook to drink
When the stars are mellow and large
  at the coming on of the night.

O, to feel the beat of the rain,
  and the homely smell of the earth,
Is a tune for the blood to jig to,
  a joy past power of words;
And the blessed green comely meadows
  are all a-ripple with mirth
At the noise of the lambs at play
  and the dear wild cry of the birds.

JOHN MASEFIELD

13

The whole world smells new. There's no one else about except the swallows sitting on the telephone wire above the village green. Just them, seven of them and me – oh – and a beady-eyed blackbird singing from the cherry tree. I've never seen so much blossom on that tree before. It's as if it's been snowing, but only on that tree and on the grass below it. It's like a little bit of winter in summer. Maybe that's what he's singing about.

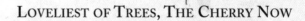

LOVELIEST OF TREES, THE CHERRY NOW

Loveliest of trees, the cherry now
Is hung with bloom along the bough,
And stands about the woodland ride
Wearing white for Eastertide.

Now, of my threescore years and ten,
Twenty will not come again,
And take from seventy springs a score,
It only leaves me fifty more.

And since to look at things in bloom
Fifty springs are little room,
About the woodlands I will go
To see the cherry hung with snow.

A. E. HOUSMAN

15

The cobbled path to the churchyard is slippy with moss, so you have to be careful. I like to go past Annie's grave and touch her gravestone.

HERE LIES ANNIE BISSET, WHO
PASSED AWAY, AGED 8
ON 15 MAY 1887
GONE, BUT NEVER FORGOTTEN.

She was exactly my age. That's why I touch the stone, so she knows I haven't forgotten.

I saw a slow-worm in here yesterday. I picked him up and smoothed him. He wasn't slimy at all. I put him in the dark under the yew tree, safe from the crows. When I go to look for him again, he's not there. Instead I find a huge golden bumblebee.

I trod on one once with my bare foot down by the river, and it stung my heel. Really hurt. This one looks stiff with cold. I let him crawl up onto the toe of my welly, and then stick shake him off in the sun, so he can get warmed up. Bees can't fly unless they're warm enough.

my painting of the village church

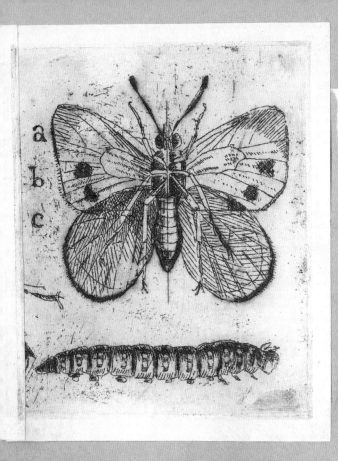

HURT NO LIVING THING

Hurt no living thing:
Ladybird, nor butterfly,
Nor moth with dusty wing,
Nor cricket chirping cheerily,
Nor grasshopper so light of leap,
Nor dancing gnat, nor beetle fat,
Nor harmless worms that creep.

CHRISTINA ROSSETTI

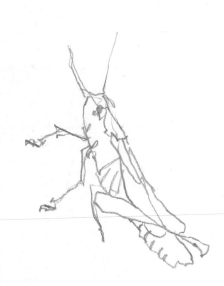

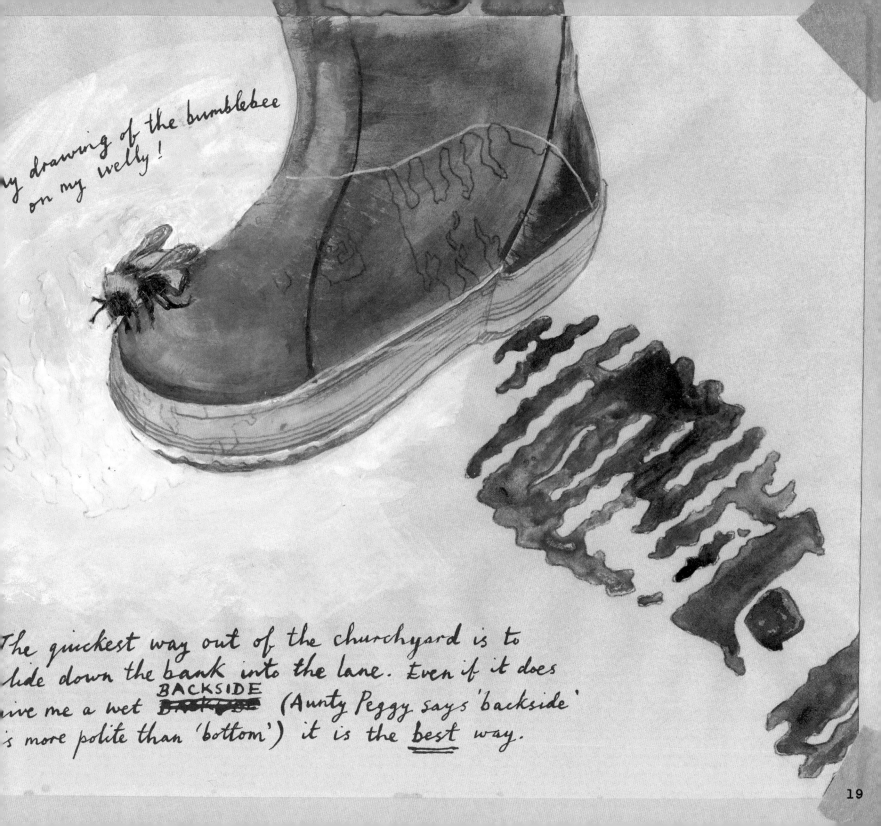

My drawing of the bumblebee on my welly!

The quickest way out of the churchyard is to slide down the bank into the lane. Even if it does give me a wet ~~BACKSIDE~~ (Aunty Peggy says 'backside' is more polite than 'bottom') it is the <u>best</u> way.

There's lambs out in the cricket field next to the village, skittering away from the gate, playing skip-and-chase. But I can see one of the ewes is on her back, her legs kicking in the air. She's in trouble. I can't just leave her, can I? The crows'll come and peck out her eyes.

The closer I come, the more she struggles, but she can't get up. I know what to do because I've seen Farmer Yelland do it.

Hands underneath and, with a great heave-ho, roll her over and up onto her feet. She's a bit wobbly, but she's fine. Her two lambs are running towards her, crying just like babies.

THE LAMB

Little Lamb, who made thee?
Dost thou know who made thee?
Gave thee life and bid thee feed
By the stream and o'er the mead;
Gave thee clothing of delight,
Softest clothing, woolly, bright;
Gave thee such a tender voice,
Making all the vales rejoice?
Little Lamb who made thee?
Dost thou know who made thee?

Little Lamb, I'll tell thee,
Little Lamb, I'll tell thee:
He is callèd by thy name,
For he calls himself a Lamb.
He is meek, and he is mild;
He became a little child.
I a child, and thou a lamb,
We are callèd by his name.
Little Lamb, God bless thee.
Little Lamb, God bless thee.

WILLIAM BLAKE

LAMB

21

The hedgerows are high on either side of me, high as the sky.
There's oak in there and blackthorn and bramble and holly and, just
past the old gateway, some dusty catkins – a nut tree too!

I HAD A LITTLE NUT TREE

I had a little nut tree,
Nothing would it bear
But a silver nutmeg
And a golden pear;

The King of Spain's daughter
Came to visit me,
And all for the sake
Of my little nut tree.

ANON

One. Two. Three. Four. I like counting and the hedgerows are perfect for it, full
of flowers and creepy-crawlies. Some days I count butterflies or spiders or
ladybirds, but this morning I'm counting flowers. Bluebells, red campions, daffodils,
primroses, dandelions, buttercups and daisies. Three hundred and twenty three, four,
five... I make it three hundred and twenty six flowers before I reach the bridge. I've
picked a dandelion clock, done my puffing and blowing. Ten o'clock.
Plenty of time.

DETERMINATION OF THE
DISTANCE TO THE MOON

51° 30' N   0° E
34° 10' S   15° 30' E

DELIGHT OF BEING ALONE

I know no greater delight than the sheer delight of being alone.
It makes me realise the delicious pleasure of the moon
that she has in travelling by herself: throughout time,
or the splendid growing of an ash-tree
alone, on a hill-side in the north, humming in the wind.

There's a ditch by the bridge full of frogspawn
great blobby glubs of it. When I look close I
can see the tadpoles wriggling about inside. "Hell
future frogs!" I tell them, just so they know.

24   D. H. LAWRENCE

THE FROG

What a wonderful bird the frog are –
When he stand, he sit almost;
When he hop, he fly almost.
He ain't got no sense hardly;
He ain't got no tail hardly either.
When he sit, he sit on what he ain't got – almost.

ANON

Frog

STICKLEBACK
STICKLEBACK

Under the trees the brook runs softly. I climb down from the
bridge, kick off my wellies so I can squish the mud and feel it
ooze between my toes. The water's freezing but I don't mind.
This is the best. If I stand here, still as a statue...

STICKLEBACK

numb. I wiggle them and the sticklebacks vanish.

STICKLEBACK

The Stickleback's a spikey chap,
    Worse than a bit of briar.
Hungry Pike would sooner swallow
    Embers from a fire.

The Stickleback is fearless in
    The way he loves his wife.
Every minute of the day
    He guards her with his life.

She, like him, is dressed to kill
    In stiff and steely prickles,
And when they kiss, there bubbles up
    The laughter of the tickles.

TED HUGHES

... the sticklebacks will come and tickle my toes.

There's two bright green dragonflies hovering over the water. I'm sure they're talking about me. They must think I'm a giant. And now the sticklebacks have arrived, nibbling away, but although I can see them, I can't feel a thing — my toes are completely

The best place to see the barn owl is sitting on the farm gate at the bottom of the track. He's often here in the early mornings or in the evenings, before it gets too dark. Maybe he just comes out when I'm here, specially for me?

It's the marshy field he likes the most – all those tasty mice
and voles in there, I expect. He doesn't come out every time,
but it's worth waiting to see if
he does. So I do.
I love owls.

And sure enough, here he is, floating down out of nowhere! He's like a white ghost,
a friendly ghost – unless you're a mouse or a vole that is. He's smaller than I
remember. He hardly moves his wings, just glides, dives once, lifts up, and then he's
gone again. I hope he caught something. He might have babies to feed. Which
reminds me, my tummy's rumbling. I wonder if there's a bun waiting for
me at the farm?

The Owl and the Pussy-Cat

The Owl and the Pussy-cat went to sea
    In a beautiful pea-green boat,
They took some honey, and plenty of money,
    Wrapped up in a five-pound note.
The Owl looked up to the stars above,
    And sang to a small guitar,
"O lovely Pussy! O Pussy, my love,
    What a beautiful Pussy you are,
        You are,
        You are!
What a beautiful Pussy you are!"

Pussy said to the Owl, "You elegant fowl!
    How charmingly sweet you sing!
O let us be married! too long we have tarried:
    But what shall we do for a ring?"
They sailed away, for a year and a day,
To the land where the Bong-tree grows,
And there in a wood a Piggy-wig stood
    With a ring at the end of his nose,
        His nose,
        His nose,
With a ring at the end of his nose.

"Dear Pig, are you willing to sell for one shilling
    Your ring?" Said the Piggy, "I will."
So they took it away, and were married next day
    By the Turkey who lives on the hill.
They dined on mince, and slices of quince,
    Which they ate with a runcible spoon.
And hand in hand, on the edge of the sand,
    They danced by the light of the moon,
        The moon,
        The moon,
They danced by the light of the moon.

Edward Lear

HIAWATHA'S CHILDHOOD

Then the little Hiawatha
Learned of every bird its language,
Learned their names and all their secrets,
How they built their nests in Summer,
Where they hid themselves in Winter,
Talked with them whene'er he met them,
Called them "Hiawatha's Chickens."

Of all beasts he learned the language,
Learned their names and all their secrets,
How the beavers built their lodges,
Where the squirrels hid their acorns,
How the reindeer ran so swiftly,
Why the rabbit was so timid,
Talked with them whene'er he met them,
Called them "Hiawatha's Brothers."

HENRY WADSWORTH LONGFELLOW

Hiawatha as a boy

Time for another dandelion clock. I blow hard this time, hard as I can. The hours float away on the air. Eleven o'clock? The sun is climbing to the top of the sky, shining down on the silvery spiders' webs strung out in the bramble hedge.

There's one spider waiting right in the middle, ~~pretending~~ pretending he's not there. Lucky I'm not a fly. I see you, spider, I see you.

INCY WINCY SPIDER

Incy Wincy spider climbed up the water spout.
Down came the rain and washed poor Incy out.
Out came the sunshine and dried up all the rain
And Incy Wincy spider climbed up the spout again.

ANON

29

A BEAUTIFUL FAT DEVON HEIFER

Which obtained a prize at Smithfield 1802, bred by Duke of Bedford.

Off up the track, and into Farmer Yelland's field, full of cows and calves. I used to be scared of cows, but I've helped bring them in so many times I'm fine with them now. They won't bother me if I don't bother them, if I keep my distance — you've got to, especially when there's calves around.

FETCHING COWS

The black one, last as usual, swings her head
And coils a black tongue round a grass-tuft. I
Watch her soft weight come down, her split feet spread.

In front, the others swing and slouch; they roll
Their great Greek eyes and breathe out milky gusts
From muzzles black and shiny as wet coal.

The collie trots, bored, at my heels, then plops
Into the ditch. The sea makes a tired sound
That's always stopping though it never stops.

A haycart squats prickeared against the sky.
Hay breath and milk breath. Far out in the West
The wrecked sun founders though its colours fly.

The collie's bored. There's nothing to control…
The black cow is two native carriers
Bringing its belly home, slung from a pole.

NORMAN MacCAIG

But the bull is out with them this morning. Samson, he's called. He hasn't hurt anyone in his life, but you never know with a bull, Farmer says. And now Samson's seen me, nodded his head at me. So I keep tight to the hedge all the way up the hill, keeping him in sight, but trying not to catch his eye. I just try to pretend he's not there. He's not there. He's not there.

Phew. I've made it to the top of the field. Best place in the world.

FROM HEREABOUT HILL

From Hereabout Hill
the sun early rising
looks over his fields
where a river runs by;
at the green of the wheat
and the green of the barley
and Candlelight Meadow
the pride of his eye.

The clock on the wall
strikes eight in the kitchen
the clock in the parlour
says twenty to nine;
the thrush has a song
and the blackbird another
· the weather reporter
says cloudless and fine.

It's green by the hedge
and white by the peartree
in Hereabout village
the date is today;
it's seven by the sun
and the time is the springtime
the first of the month and
the month must be May.

SEÁN RAFFERTY

But now the cows are on the move, so are the calves and so's Samson, climbing up, coming my way. Mustn't run, mustn't run. They won't hurt me. He won't hurt me. But I'll get to the other side of that gate quick!

My heart's going like a train. I reach out to scratch their foreheads as they say hello, breathe the smell of them, stare back into Samson's eye, all from the other side of the gate. Very brave, I am.

33

Down I go into the dip towards the farmhouse. The pigs are out in the yard. Farmer lets his pigs wander all over the place. That's what they like best, he says. He talks to his animals like he talks to people. That's why I like him. Sarah-Jane's his favourite sow and she's been ~~and~~ rolling in puddles, caked in mud, hardly pink at all any more. There are eight little piglets chasing around after her. Eight out of nine. Last time I was here we found one of them dead. Sarah-Jane must have lain on him and squashed him by mistake. We buried that little pig in the orchard, Farmer and me, ~~put~~ put primroses on the grave – Farmer's favourite flower, mine too.

THIS LITTLE PIG

This little pig went to market,
This little pig stayed at home,
This little pig had roast beef,
This little pig had none,
And this little pig cried
"Wee, wee, wee!"
All the way home.

ANON

Farmer gives me lemonade and a sticky bun, more than one sometimes. Today I have two, wolf them down, but we don't hang about in his kitchen. Farmer likes me coming round - I think - but he doesn't like to have to talk too much. He likes to get on.

love to help him, it makes me feel useful.
e wants me to fetch in logs from the wood-
ed ... Dark in there. I make a
t of noise, so that whatever's
ding can hear me coming
nd run off.

A SMALL DRAGON

I've found a small dragon in the woodshed.
Think it must have come from deep inside a forest
because it's damp and green and leaves
are still reflecting in its eyes.

I fed it on many things, tried grass,
the roots of stars, hazel-nut and dandelion,
but it stared up at me as if to say, I need
foods you can't provide.

It made a nest among the coal,
not unlike a bird's but larger,
it is out of place here
and is mosttimes silent.

If you believed in it I would come
hurrying to your house to let you share this wonder,
but I want instead to see
if you yourself will pass this way.

BRIAN PATTEN

Farmer says I can take Captain out if I like, so long as I groom him and pick out his hooves before I go. Captain's coat is full of dust, so he takes a lot of grooming. He treads on my toe and swishes me in the face with his tail. Thanks a lot, Captain. But he's not being nasty, just letting me know that he wants to go out, that he's fed up with being groomed.

As soon as I put the saddle on him he's happy, and as I swing myself up and we walk out of the farmyard, he's happier still. Past the duck pond; five ducks, ten ducklings, two geese, one gosling and the moorhen. That's good, same as before. Looks like the fox has stayed away.

Twelve's coming along with us too, so excited his tail's whirling round like a propeller.

I even managed a handy bark
At the dog on the next farm, over four fields
And got a good boy for it.
Cows' heels were just starters warming me up –
I could do it with my tongue idling.
Serious at sheep was how I earned my keep
Working my master's face
Through all its shapes, without a mistake,
Getting his arms right each time
And making his whistle easy.
My ears fairly ached
At stopping and starting.
I had every single mutton helpless
Under my ideas.

DOG

I dreamed I woke and was a bark
Working at the postman and the boy
With the newspaper. I watched hard
My master's breakfast mouth,
Sitting with all my might.
With all my skill I caught
The bacon-rind and did for it –
Clapping my chops to make a neat job.
When he stood I was so quick
Already standing, and my tail turning over
Without a problem. On the way
I checked every sniff – Good morning! Good morning!

I threw in a few dodges –
Spinning them on one hoof,
Rolling the flock up on three sides at once
Like a pasty,
Pouring them through a nozzle.
I made a point
Of snatching a good boy
From under the tail of each one.
My panting
Finally used all the work up,

And daylight had to go.
I ate a bowl of good boy
Still keeping my master's eyes safe,
And resting his footsteps in my right ear
Till I slept.
Believe me, I slept without a pause
Even when the sleep-wolf
Jeering at me, dashed through my skin
Like a clock-alarm.

TED HUGHES

41

He's called Twelve, because he's the twelfth sheepdog Farmer has had. He's a champion sheepdog, knows every one of the sheep, by name almost, Farmer says. But when Twelve's out with me, he goes loopy, running round in circles, chasing his tail, chasing anything — hens are his favourite. Loopy.

FERN HILL

Now as I was young and easy under the apple boughs
About the lilting house and happy as the grass was green,
   The night above the dingle starry,
    Time let me hail and climb
   Golden in the heydays of his eyes,
And honoured among wagons I was prince of the apple towns
And once below a time I lordly had the trees and leaves
    Trail with daisies and barley
   Down the rivers of the windfall light.

And as I was green and carefree, famous among the barns
About the happy yard and singing as the farm was home,
   In the sun that is young once only,
    Time let me play and be
   Golden in the mercy of his means,
And green and golden I was huntsman and herdsman, the calves
Sang to my horn, the foxes on the hills barked clear and cold,
    And the sabbath rang slowly
   In the pebbles of the holy streams.

DYLAN THOMAS

Out in Oak Meadow, there's only the stump of a tree left now, right in the middle. Farmer says it was a great oak tree once, huge, older than my grandpa, and my grandpa's grandpa, and his grandpa too probably.

This is the Man who planted Trees

(by Jean Giono)

and his dog

Acorns

I stroke Captain's ears, give him a pat and a bit of a gee-up. Captain only does walking, a bit like me. He never does trotting. It suits me fine. Up here, rocking away, I can see the whole of the sky. There's a bunch of crows chasing two buzzards out of the trees. They mew like cats, buzzards, if you listen. <u>Why can't you leave them alone</u> I shake my fist at the crows. Only one bird worse than a crow, and that's a magpie Aunty Peggy always spits and salutes when she sees a magpie. For luck, she says. I do it myself now, just in case there's one about. You never know, do you?

THE MAGPIE RHYME

One for sorrow, two for joy,
Three for a girl, four for a boy,
Five for silver, six for gold,
Seven for a secret never to be told,
Eight for a letter over the sea,
Nine for a lover as true as can be.

ANON

45

As we come up to the top of Penny Hill, there's a hare right in front of us, just sitting there. A hare sits taller than a rabbit, stiller, and he's browner. And when he runs he goes, well... like a hare, jinking and weaving, till he weaves himself into the long grass and he's gone.

HARES AT PLAY

The birds are gone to bed the cows are still
And sheep lie panting on each old mole hill
And underneath the willows grey-green bough
Like toil a-resting – lies the fallow plough
The timid hares throw daylights fears away
On the lanes road to dust and dance and play
Then dabble in the grain by nought deterred
To lick the dew fall from the barleys beard
Then out they sturt again and round the hill
Like happy thoughts – dance – squat – and loiter still
Till milking maidens in the early morn
Jingle their yokes and sturt them in the corn
Through well known beaten paths each nimbling hare
Starts quick as fear – and seeks its hidden lair

JOHN CLARE

Captain knows the way, down the hill and into Bluebell Wood—
Jabberwocky country, bear country, ghost country, particularly
when the wind's whooing through the trees. But there's no wind today.
No Jabberwockys, no bears, no ghosts. Only me.

I'm keeping my eye out for deer, leaping the brook maybe, or the whitey back-end of one running through the shadows. I've seen them often in Bluebell Wood, and badgers too – playing in the evenings at the top of the slope. But not today. There's foxes in here though. I can smell them. They can smell me too, that's for sure. There's one looking at me right now, I expect. In Bluebell Wood I feel there's eyes looking at me all the time. So long as it's not a Jabberwocky or a bear or a ghost...There's a jay cackling away at me out of sight. Hope it's a jay and not a witch.

Bluebells aren't blue when they're all together in their hundreds and thousands like this. ~~They~~ They're purple, and they smell purple too.

47

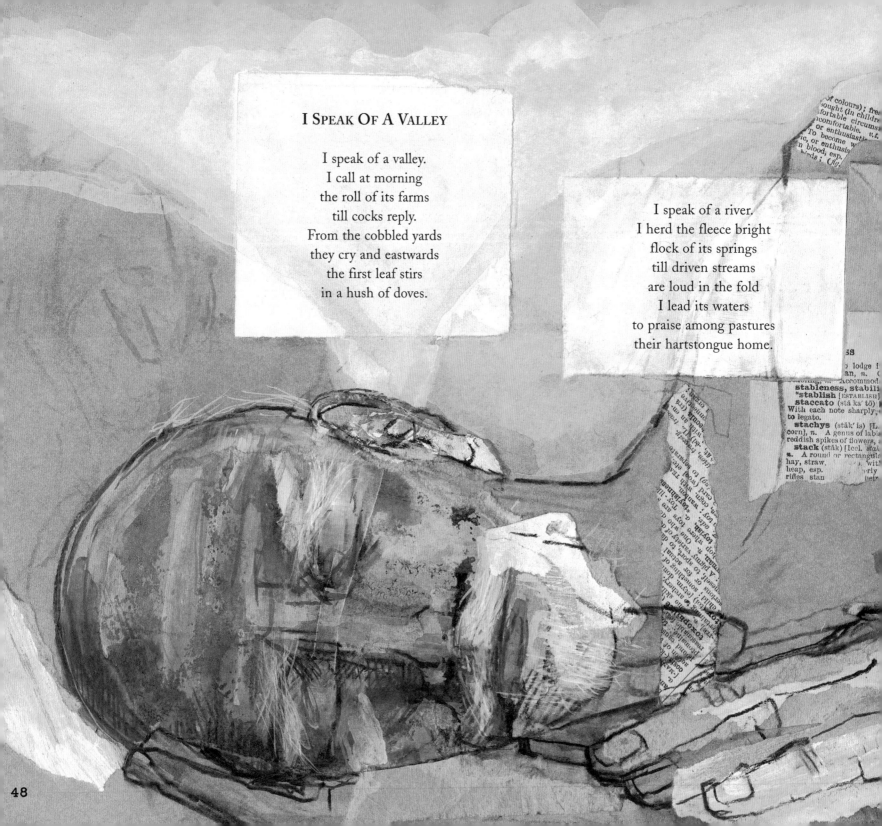

I Speak Of A Valley

I speak of a valley.
I call at morning
the roll of its farms
till cocks reply.
From the cobbled yards
they cry and eastwards
the first leaf stirs
in a hush of doves.

I speak of a river.
I herd the fleece bright
flock of its springs
till driven streams
are loud in the fold
I lead its waters
to praise among pastures
their hartstongue home.

I speak of a childhood.
I lay a nightlong
fable of sleep
till morning sang
in the green of the light
between leaf and language
a birth of ballad
a bird alone.

Ballad and childhood
and psalm and river
in the cup of my hands
I priest its praise;
I speak of a valley
and shall for ever
out of my numbered days.

SEÁN RAFFERTY

Captain likes to stop for a drink in the river. So I slide off him, and go stone-skimming while he has a good slurp. Skimming's not easy today, because the river's running too fast, there are too many ripples. My record is fifteen but three hops is all I can manage now. After a while I give up and just sit there under the shade of the willows. This is the place I do my best dreaming, my best thinking.

The little dipper's there, diving into the river from his stone, then he pops out again, shaking his feathers dry, and off.

A kingfisher! A kingfisher flashes by and he's gone, almost before I even saw him, his colours so bright that they stay in my head long after he's gone.

KINGFISHER

That kingfisher jewelling upstream
seems to leave a streak of itself
in the bright air. The trees
are all the better for its passing.

It's not a mineral eater, though it looks it.
It doesn't nip nicks out of the edges
of rainbows. – It dives
into the burly water, then, perched
on a Japanese bough, gulps
into its own incandescence
a wisp of minnow, a warrior stickleback.
– Or it vanishes into its burrow, resplendent
Samurai, returning home
to his stinking slum.

NORMAN MacCAIG

KINGFISHER

That kingfisher jewelling upstream
seems to leave a streak of itself
in the bright air. The trees
are all the better for its passing.

It's not a mineral eater, though it looks it.
It doesn't nip nicks out of the edges
of rainbows. — It dives
into the burly water, then, perched
on a Japanese bough, gulps
into its own incandescence
a wisp of minnow, a warrior stickleback.
— Or it vanishes into its burrow, resplendent
Samurai, returning home
to his stinking slum.

NORMAN MACCAIG

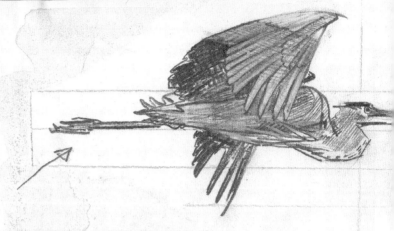

Everything is so peaceful, so still, and that's when I see the heron. I hardly ~~dare~~ dare breathe. He's stalking in slow motion through the shallows, looking for fish. He's stock-still now, waiting to strike. But then Twelve, who's been busy chasing rabbits, comes bounding over the bank. The heron lifts off at once, soaring away on his wide, wide wings. He flies like a pterodactyl. Thanks a lot, Twelve. Thanks a lot.

There are otter tracks in the mud. I follow them along the water's edge, and soon enough I find what I'm looking for, otter poo – 'spraint', Aunty Peggy calls it, because poo is another word she doesn't like. I have a good sniff. Quite fresh, bony, fishy, oily. He must have been here last night. I've only ever seen an otter once, and it was right here. I'm always praying to see another one... but it's only a squirrel, skittering along the ground and up the trunk of the tree beside me. Why do they twitch their tails like they do?

To a Squirrel at Kyle-Na-No

Come play with me;
Why should you run
Through the shaking tree
As though I'd a gun
To strike you dead?
When all I would do
Is to scratch your head
And let you go.

W. B. Yeats

The dandelion clock says two o'clock, time for lunch. It must be about right, because the sun's beginning to lower itself. Captain's nudging me. He wants to get moving, he wants to go home. I make him stand in the river and jump on from the bank. High enough now to see there's someone there, fishing on the other side of the river.

He doesn't say a word as we ride past, doesn't even look at us. So I say hello very loudly and give him a big wave, just to annoy him. I recognise him now. I've seen him out hunting on his big black horse, in his bright red jacket. His cheeks are the same colour.

I Saw a Jolly Hunter

I saw a jolly hunter
With a jolly gun
Walking in the country
In the jolly sun.

In the jolly meadow
Sat a jolly hare.
Saw the jolly hunter.
Took jolly care.

Hunter jolly eager –
Sight of jolly prey.
Forgot gun pointing
Wrong jolly way.

Jolly hunter jolly head
Over heels gone.
Jolly old safety catch
Not jolly on.

Bang went the jolly gun.
Hunter jolly dead.
Jolly hare got clean away.
Jolly good, I said.

CHARLES CAUSLEY

I wonder if he can see the cross from his side
of the river - for all the fishes that have ever
been caught, all the foxes that have ever
been hunted?

I once saw a huge salmon, shining silver in
the sun and fighting for its life on the end of
a line. That fish came all the way from the sea,
thousands of miles, travelling right back up the

river to the place it was born. They do that. Like swallows or homing pigeons. And after all those miles, all that effort, the salmon gets himself dragged out of the river with a hook in his mouth.

I ride on fast. I don't want to be near if he catches another one today.

There's millions of cowpats in Marsh Field. Dry ones, hard-baked, so hard you could pick one up and throw it like a discus. Or that's what I thought until I tried it one day. The cowpat I'd chosen wasn't hard-enough-baked, and when I picked it up, I got my fingers covered in gunk – it stank like anything. I ran down to the river and plunged in my hand to wash it off. I kept plunging and washing till my hand was as clean as a whistle. But it went on smelling for days afterwards.

One thing's for sure, I won't do discus-throwing with cowpats ever again.

Cow II

The Cow is but a bagpipe,
All bag, all bones, all blort.
They bawl me out of bed at dawn
And never give a thought
    a thought
They never give a thought.

The milk-herd is a factory:
Milk, meat, butter, cheese.
You think these come in rivers? O
The slurry comes in seas
     seas
The slurry comes in seas.

A cowclap is an honest job,
A black meringue for the flies.
But when the sea of slurry spills
Your shining river dies
     dies
Your shining river dies.

Say this about cows:
Nothing can stop
From one end the Moo
From t'other the flop
    flop
    flop
    flippety-flop
Floppety-flippety.

TED HUGHES

I ride back to the farm the long way because I want my ride to last as long as possible. Through the oak forest I'll go...

60

...then up the stony track where Aunty Peggy brings me blackberry picking, right up to the haunted cottage, which looks as if it's been shut up for a hundred years. It makes me shiver.

The Listeners

"Is there anybody there?" said the Traveller,
Knocking on the moonlit door;
And his horse in the silence champed the grasses
Of the forest's ferny floor,
And a bird flew up out of the turret,
Above the Traveller's head:
And he smote upon the door again a second time;
"Is there anybody there?" he said.
But no one descended to the Traveller;
No head from the leaf-fringed sill
Leaned over and looked into his grey eyes,
Where he stood perplexed and still.
But only a host of phantom listeners
That dwelt in the lone house then
Stood listening in the quiet of the moonlight
To that voice from the world of men:
Stood thronging the faint moonbeams on the dark stair
That goes down to the empty hall,
Hearkening in an air stirred and shaken
By the lonely Traveller's call.
And he felt in his heart their strangeness,
Their stillness answering his cry,
While his horse moved, cropping the dark turf,
'Neath the starred and leafy sky;
For he suddenly smote on the door, even
Louder, and lifted his head: –
"Tell them I came, and no one answered,
That I kept my word," he said.
Never the least stir made the listeners,
Though every word he spake
Fell echoing through the shadowiness of the still house
From the one man left awake:
Aye, they heard his foot upon the stirrup,
And the sound of iron on stone,
And how the silence surged softly backward,
When the plunging hoofs were gone.

WALTER DE LA MARE

STOPPING BY WOODS ON A SNOWY EVENING

Whose woods these are I think I know.
His house is in the village though;
He will not see me stopping here
To watch his woods fill up with snow.

My little horse must think it queer
To stop without a farmhouse near
Between the woods and frozen lake
The darkest evening of the year.

He gives his harness bells a shake
To ask if there is some mistake.
The only other sound's the sweep
Of easy wind and downy flake.

The woods are lovely, dark and deep,
But I have promises to keep,
And miles to go before I sleep,
And miles to go before I sleep.

ROBERT FROST

High up on Captain, I can see over the hedges. Farmer is out on his tractor, Little Grey Fergie – he loves that tractor, the best he's ever had, he says. I bet he's singing too. Being on his tractor makes him sing. He's rolling the grass field, making it stripy, like a football pitch. He'll be cutting it for hay in a couple of months or so. Depends on the weather. Everything on the farm depends on the weather. He's told me that often enough.

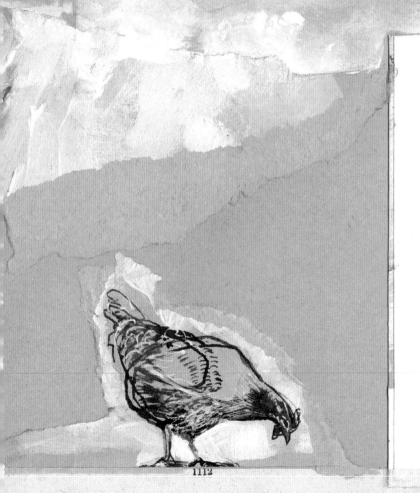

CYNDDYLAN ON A TRACTOR

Ah, you should see Cynddylan on a tractor.
Gone the old look that yoked him to the soil;
He's a new man now, part of the machine,
His nerves of metal and his blood oil.
The clutch curses, but the gears obey
His least bidding, and lo, he's away
Out of the farmyard, scattering hens.
Riding to work now as a great man should,
He is the knight at arms breaking the fields'
Mirror of silence, emptying the wood
Of foxes and squirrels and bright jays.
The sun comes over the tall trees
Kindling all the hedges, but not for him
Who runs his engine on a different fuel.
And all the birds are singing, bills wide in vain,
As Cynddylan passes proudly up the lane.

R. S. THOMAS

Captain walks on faster with every step, his head nodding away. He's a funny old horse. First he can't wait to get out of his stable, then once he's out he can't wait to get back. I couldn't stop him now even if I wanted to. We're almost trotting by the time we get back in the yard. ~~At~~ Almost, but not quite.

The hens and ducks scatter as we come riding in, Twelve barking his head off, just letting them know who's boss.

CHICKEN

Clapping her platter stood plump Bess,
And all across the green
Came scampering in, on wing and claw,
Chicken fat and lean:
Dorking, Spaniard, Cochin China,
Bantams sleek and small,
Like feathers blown in a great wind,
They came at Bessie's call.

WALTER DE LA MARE

Captain whinnies loudly, telling the whole world he's back. Barnaby, the donkey, brays back to him from the patch of dusty nettles by the barn. Maybe horse and donkey speak the same language, if only I could understand.

DONKEY

Is an ancient colour. He's the colour
Of a prehistoric desert
Where great prehistoric suns have sunk and burned out
To a blueish powder.

He stood there through it all, head hanging.

He's the colour
Of a hearth-full of ashes, next morning,
Tinged with rusty pink.

Or the colour of a cast-iron donkey, roasted in a bonfire,
And still standing there after it, cooling,
Pale with ashes and oxides.

He's been through a lot.

But here he is in the nettles, under the chestnut leaves,
With his surprising legs,
Such useful ready legs, so light and active.

And neat round hooves, for putting down just anywhere,
Ready to start out again this minute scrambling all over Tibet!

And his quite small body, tough and tight and
    useful,
Like traveller's luggage,
A thing specially made for hard use, with no
    trimmings,
Nearly ugly. Made to outlast its owner.

His face is what I like.
And his head, much too big for his body – a toy head,
A great, rabbit-eared, pantomime head,
And his friendly rabbit face,
His big, friendly, humorous eyes – which can turn wicked,
Long and devilish, when he lays his ears back.

But mostly he's comical – and that's what I like.
I like the joke he seems
Always just about to tell me. And the laugh,
The rusty, pump-house engine that cranks up laughter
From some long-ago, far-off, laughterless desert –

The dry, hideous guffaw
That makes his great teeth nearly fall out.

TED HUGHES

Greetings from the Himalayas

67

As soon as Captain's saddle's off and hung up, I give him lots of hugs and pats and, what he's waiting for, a handful of barleycorn. He can't wait, he snuffles it up with his whiskery, rubbery lips.

Barley's his favourite.

RISE UP AGAIN (BARLEYCORN)

Cruel winter cuts through like The Reaper
The old year lies withered and slain
And like Barleycorn who rose from the grave
A new year will rise up again.

And the snow falls – the wind calls
The year turns round again
And like Barleycorn who rose from the grave
A new year will rise up again.

And I'll wager a hat full of guineas
Against all of the songs you can sing
Some day you'll love and the next day you'll lose
And winter will turn into spring.

Ploughed and sown – reaped and mown
The year turns round again
And like Barleycorn who rose from the grave
A new year will rise up again.

I will garland a bonnet of daisies
To crown you the Queen of the May
And all shall behold the seasons unfold
As surely as night follows day.

Phoebe arise – a gleam in her eyes
The year turns round again
And like Barleycorn who rose from the grave
A new year will rise up again.

But there will come a time of great plenty
A time of good harvest and sun
Till then put your trust in tomorrow my friend
For yesterday's over and done.

And the snow falls – the wind calls
The year turns round again
And like Barleycorn who rose from the grave
A new year will rise up again.

JOHN TAMS

71

Farmer's washing his hands when I go in, and he makes me wash mine. Fish pie for lunch. We don't talk much while we're eating. "Got something I thought you'd like to see, Pippa," he says afterwards. It's a huge beetle in a matchbox, bluey-black and shiny. "I found him near the ~~the~~ dungheap. Nearly got himself eaten by a hen. You can let him out if you like, on your way home."

He knows I like little creatures, But he doesn't know that sometimes I like them so much I hang on to them for a while. I haven't told anyone that I keep them hidden in the bottom drawer in the cupboard in my bedroom at Aunty Peggy's.

I've had all sorts in there. hedgehog, slow-worm, shrew, even a grass snake once. I let them go in the end of course, sometimes in the churchyard where there's plenty of long grass to hide in.

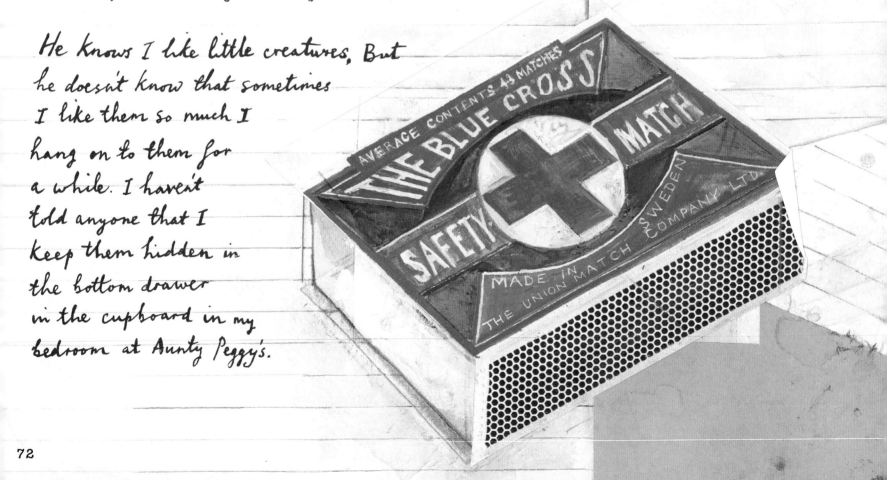

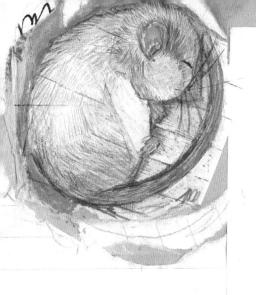

THE MEADOW MOUSE

In a shoe box stuffed in an old nylon stocking
Sleeps the baby mouse I found in the meadow,
Where he trembled and shook beneath a stick
Till I caught him up by the tail and brought him in,
Cradled in my hand,
A little quaker, the whole body of him trembling,
His absurd whiskers sticking out like a cartoon-mouse,
His feet like small leaves,
Little lizard-feet,
Whitish and spread wide when he tried to struggle away,
Wriggling like a minuscule puppy.

Now he's eaten his three kinds of cheese and drunk
from his bottle-cap watering-trough –
So much he just lies in one corner,
His tail curled under him, his belly big
As his head; his bat-like ears
Twitching, tilting toward the least sound.
Do I imagine he no longer trembles
When I come close to him?
He seems no longer to tremble.

But this morning the shoe-box house on the back porch is empty.
Where has he gone, my meadow mouse,
My thumb of a child that nuzzled in my palm? –
To run under the hawk's wing,
Under the eye of the great owl watching from the elm-tree,
To live by courtesy of the shrike, the snake, the tom-cat.

I think of the nestling fallen into the deep grass,
The turtle gasping in the dusty rubble of the highway,
The paralytic stunned in the tub, and the water rising, –
All things innocent, hapless, forsaken.

THEODORE ROETHKE

"You'd better get home now," says Farmer. "I got my digging to do. Earth needs turning over, needs to breathe, just like we do."

He doesn't like goodbyes, nor do I, nor does Captain. So off I go. When I look back, he's already at his digging.

Seems Farmer isn't the only one out digging his garden today. As I wander down the lane past Duck's Lake Cottage I hear the sound of someone ~~sing~~ singing behind the hedge. I climb up and have a look. Old Les is out in his vegetable patch and he's digging too. I wave and he waves. Then he's back to his singing and his digging under the apple trees.

Between my finger & thumb my

The squat pen rests. snug as a gun

Under my window a clean rasping sound

When the spade sinks into the gravelly groun

... off hinges ... runs funny off

Bents low, comes up twenty years

in rhythm through potato

... buried the bright edge deep

... man could handle a spade;

75

Les says that they used to sing to the apple trees
so that they'd be sure to give a good harvest.
Singing and dancing all night under the trees.

WALK THIS WORLD WITH MUSIC

Starry night and
starry night and
we were brave and
we were bright and
as we sang
with all our might
the moon came out
to cheer us

this will go on
though dynasties pass
to mark and circumscribe our listless lives
the staff of life in crumbs may fall
but we will walk this world
with music

The orchards rang
the orchards rang
their muskets rattle
our saucepans bang
and as we gathered and
as we sang
the year came in
to cheer us

A perfect day
a perfect day
the last of April
the first of May
and
as we dance and as we play
the sun comes up
to cheer us

this will go on
though dynasties pass
to mark and circumscribe our listless lives
the staff of life in crumbs may fall
but we will walk this world
with music

A final day
a final day and
how your breath it slips
away and
as we sing your chosen hymn
we stand
and wonder
can you hear us?

this will go on
though dynasties pass
to mark and circumscribe our listless lives
the staff of life in crumbs will fall
but We Will Walk this World
with music

CHRIS WOOD

79

At the end of the farm lane I pick another dandelion clock. Home time, it says. I set off down the hill, towards the bridge. I'm not far along the road when I see the lizard, right in the middle, ~~&~~ and he's a big one too. I crouch down over him. He's half asleep, basking in the sun. I talk to him, telling him he'll get squashed if he doesn't move, trying to shoo him on, but he won't budge. So I reach out and touch his back. That's when he wakes up, and with a twitch of his tail he's gone into the ditch. That's my good deed for the day!

WHERE THE BEE SUCKS, THERE SUCK I

Where the bee sucks, there suck I:
In a cowslip's bell I lie;
There I couch when owls do cry.
On the bat's back I do fly
After summer merrily.
Merrily, merrily shall I live now
Under the blossom that hangs on the bough.

WILLIAM SHAKESPEARE

I stand on the bridge for a while
and play pooh sticks.

81

There aren't any dragonflies any more, but I can see lots of butterflies. Butterflies are what I'll count, all the way back up the hill to the village, beginning right now:

1   Holly Blue

Celastrina Argiolus

2   Large white

Pieris Brassicae

3   Common Blue bu

four peacock butterflies, five red admirals and two tiny blue ones, so beautiful, flying around one another, dancing in the air.

4   Peacock butterfly

Inachis Io

5   Small Tortoiseshel.

Aglais urticae

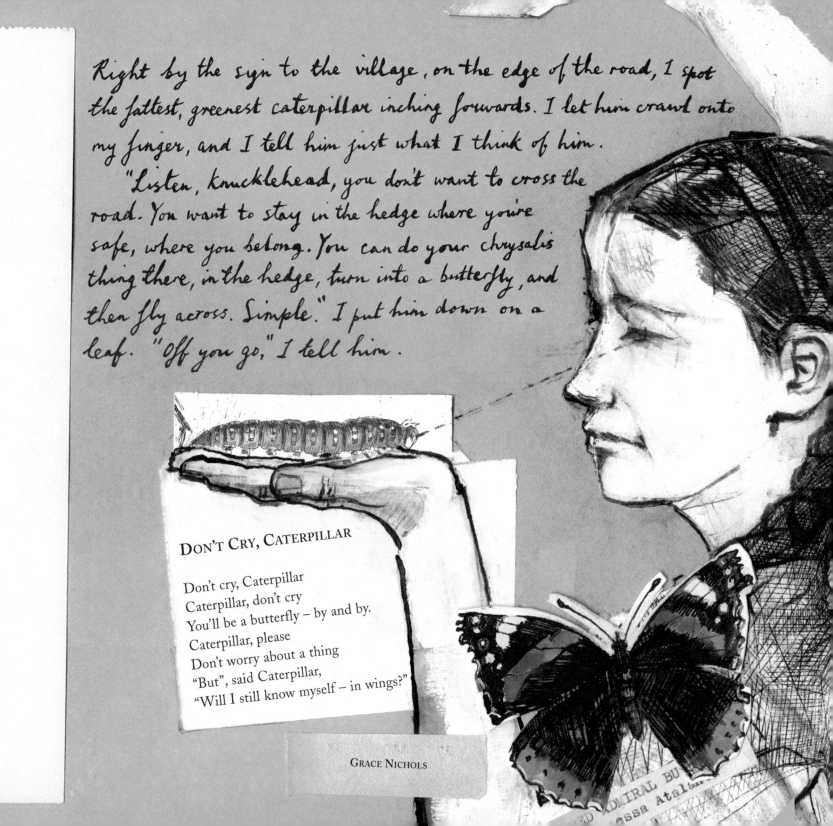

Right by the sign to the village, on the edge of the road, I spot the fattest, greenest caterpillar inching forwards. I let him crawl onto my finger, and I tell him just what I think of him.

"Listen, knucklehead, you don't want to cross the road. You want to stay in the hedge where you're safe, where you belong. You can do your chrysalis thing there, in the hedge, turn into a butterfly, and then fly across. Simple." I put him down on a leaf. "Off you go," I tell him.

DON'T CRY, CATERPILLAR

Don't cry, Caterpillar
Caterpillar, don't cry
You'll be a butterfly – by and by.
Caterpillar, please
Don't worry about a thing
"But", said Caterpillar,
"Will I still know myself – in wings?"

GRACE NICHOLS

There's hundreds of crows out in the field below the village and I'm not the only one who hates them, everyone does. Farmer Yelland hates them because they eat his corn and they peck out his lambs' eyes. Aunty Peggy hates them because they rob birds' nests, killing everything – baby robins, baby blackbirds, baby wagtails.

LITTLE TROTTY WAGTAIL

Little trotty wagtail he went in the rain
And tittering tottering sideways he near got straight again
He stooped to get a worm and look'd up to catch a fly
And then he flew away e're his feathers they were dry

Little trotty wagtail he waddled in the mud
And left his little foot marks trample where he would
He waddled in the water pudge and waggle went his tail
And chirrup up his wings to dry upon the garden rail

Little trotty wagtail you nimble all about
And in the dimpling water pudge you waddle in and out
Your home is nigh at hand and in the warm pigsty
So little Master Wagtail I'll bid you a goodbye

JOHN CLARE

BLOW

Farmer Yelland's got a saying about crows, about how clever they are: "A crow always knows, 'cos a crow's got a nose for knowing."

Dandelion clock says it's one o'clock again. That can't be right. Must be later than that.

As I come up into the village the church bells are ringing, and they shouldn't be. It's not Sunday is it? And there's music playing too, a band, the silver band. I can hear the big bass drum banging away.

And there was the band with that curious tone
Of the cornet, clarinet and big trombone
Fiddle, 'cello, big bass drum
Bassoon, flute and euphonium
Each one making the most of his chance
All together in the Floral Dance.

I felt so lonely standing there
And I could only stand and stare
For I had no boy with me
Lonely I should have to be
In that quaint old Cornish town

When suddenly hast'ning down the lane
A figure I knew I saw quite plain
With outstretched hands he came along
And carried me into that merry throng
And fiddle and all went dancing down.

We danced to the band with the curious tone
Of the cornet, clarinet and big trombone
Fiddle, 'cello, big bass drum
Bassoon, flute and euphonium
Each one making the most of his chance
Altogether in the Floral Dance.

Dancing here, prancing there
Jigging, jogging ev'rywhere
Up and down, and round the town
Hurrah! For the Cornish Floral Dance.

KATE EMILY MOSS

THE FLORAL DANCE

As I walked home on a summer night
When stars in heav'n were shining bright
Far away from the footlight's glare
Into the sweet and scented air
Of a quaint old Cornish town

Borne from afar on the gentle breeze
Joining the murmur of the summer seas
Distant tones of an old world dance
Played by the village band perchance
On the calm air came floating down.

I thought I could hear the curious tone
Of the cornet, clarinet and big trombone
Fiddle, 'cello, big bass drum
Bassoon, flute and euphonium
Far away, as in a trance
I heard the sound of the Floral Dance.

And soon I heard such a bustling and prancing
And then I saw the whole village was dancing
In and out of the houses they came
Old folk, young folk, all the same
In that quaint old Cornish town.

Every boy took a girl 'round the waist
And hurried her off in tremendous haste
Whether they knew one another I care not
Whether they cared at all, I know not
But they kissed as they danced along.

There's flags flying everywhere, and I can smell cooking. What's going on? I come round the corner. There's hundreds of people out on the village green, and they're all looking at me, smiling and clapping. Aunty Peggy's there too, shaking her head at me, but she's not cross. "Well done, Pippa," she's saying. "You're the first back. Amazing! Miraculous! Incredible! Three miles in under two minutes. The others are miles behind, even the grown-up runners. You've won, and what's more, you've done it in your wellies too!"

I'd been in my own world all day and completely forgotten about it. The race! Of course, the race. That's what I didn't want to be back for by four o'clock! It's May Day, the Round the Island Road race, all three miles of it. It puffs me out, makes my legs ache, and I don't see the point of it anyway, unless you win, which I never ever d

Until now!

The finishing tape's right there ahead of me and they're all cheering me on, the whole village! I'm running now, and funnily enough I'm not puffed and my legs don't hurt at all. I'm going for the finishing tape, arms raised like an Olympic champion, an Olympic champion in wellies!

The tape wraps around me, and I'm laughing, and the whole world's laughing with me.

PIPPA'S SONG

The year's at the spring,
And day's at the morn;
Morning's at seven;
The hill-side's dew-pearl'd;
The lark's on the wing;
The snail's on the thorn;
God's in His heaven –
All's right with the world!

ROBERT BROWNING

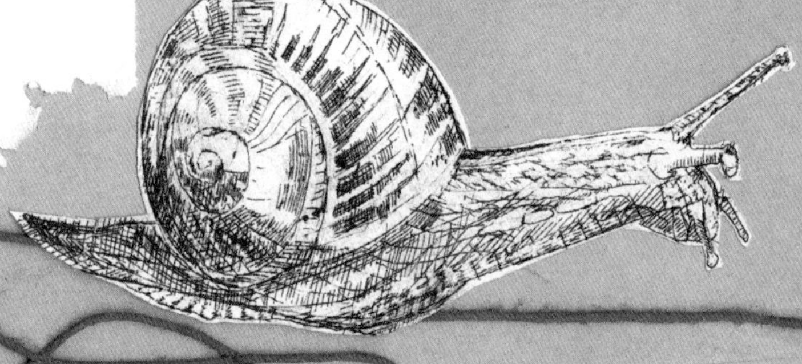

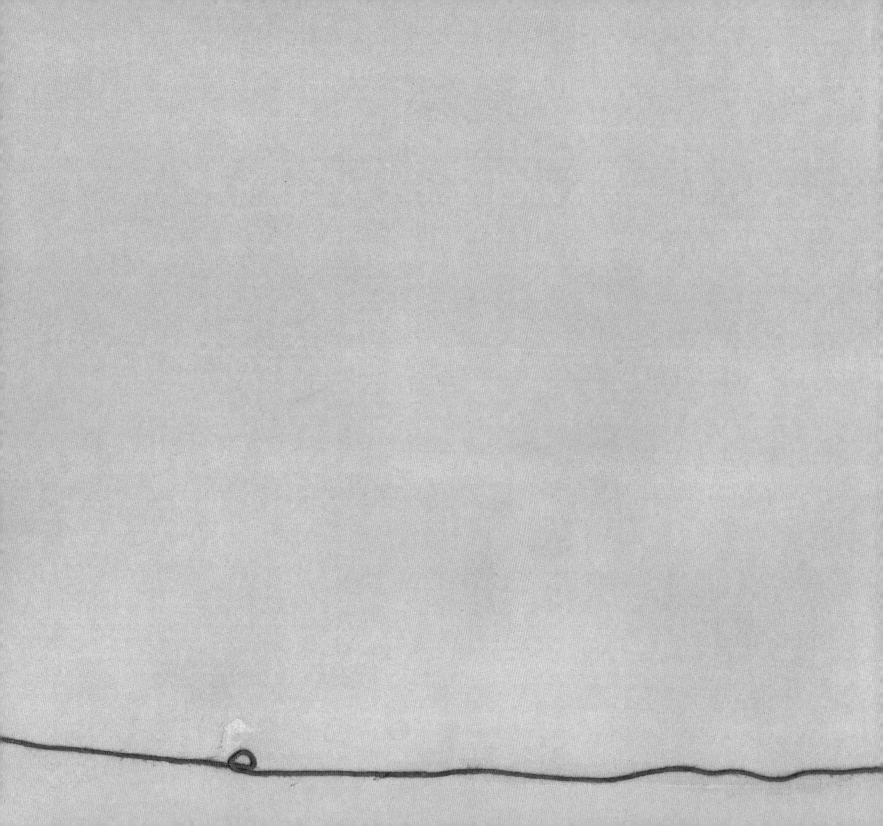

THE STORY OF
THIS BOOK

Where My Wellies Take Me owes its inspiration to many people who have been strong influences in the lives of Clare and Michael Morpurgo. At school in the '50s Clare was encouraged by her Head Mistress Monica Brookes to learn a new poem by heart every week. Michael's mother, Kippe, read poetry to him at bedtime, before she turned off the light and kissed him goodnight. Many of the poems in this book come from these years and are now like old friends, always welcomed with a smile of recognition. Growing up in the countryside, both children were soaking up their experiences and storing them away in their imaginations, for the future.

Clare's father, Allen Lane, founder of Penguin Books and devoted to Devon, brought Clare to Iddesleigh in the late '40s. He introduced her to some old friends, Peggy and Seán Rafferty, who had left London after the Second World War and had come to run a pub, the Duke of York, in the village. They invited the little girl (pictured here) to come and spend her holidays with them and their daughter. Seán was a poet and some of his poems appear in this book.

Frequent visitors to the Duke of York were Ted Hughes and his wife Carol. Much later, Clare and Michael – who were married by this point – came to live near the village in order to set up Farms for City Children. The three couples became the best of friends and this friendship nurtured much of the creative work of the three writers. Living in Iddesleigh inspired Michael to write War Horse, Farm Boy and Private Peaceful.

Although Clare always read the first draft of each new book and had typed many of them, the couple had never collaborated on a book before. So when, in 2009, their close friend and adviser Philippa Perry suggested to Amanda Wood, the Creative Director at Templar, that they might work on a book together, to be sold in aid of Farms for City Children, everyone was delighted.

The original idea was to create a collection of animal poems, but in the end Clare and Michael came up with the idea of a book of poems about the countryside, with a new story by Michael to link the poems. This story would follow the character of Pippa, and be loosely based on Clare's childhood walks in and around the village of Iddesleigh. All that was needed now was an illustrator, and here fate stepped in again.

Fine artist Olivia Lomenech Gill, visiting her family-in-law in Brittany with her husband and two small sons, happened to be at a festival of young people's books in the little fishing port of Doëlan when an eager organiser said she must meet "the very famous English author we have here". Despite Olivia's protestations – "we are definitely not going to go and say hello just because we are from England!" – the organiser wouldn't take no for an answer. Luckily, the Morpurgos and Olivia hit it off immediately and, upon discovering they were booked on the same ferry home, arranged to dine together on the boat. It was then that Michael asked to see Olivia's sketchbook.

Three months later, Michael showed Olivia a draft of Pippa's story, as well as a wad of various poems, all photocopied from different sources. She started work straightaway, in her head at least: "I found myself thinking, 'Why are the poems there?' and it seemed clear to me from the beginning that Pippa had put them there. It was her book, a holiday journal but set in real time, one day in Devon."

Having received the go-ahead from Mike Jolley, Templar's Art Director, Olivia travelled to Iddesleigh in May 2010 in order to be there for the May Day celebrations. She witnessed the finish of the Round the Island Race, which still takes place every May Day in Iddesleigh. Camping in the Morpurgos' garden, with Michael's scribbled-on Ordnance Survey map as her guide, over the next few days she put together, piece-by-piece, the walk that Pippa had done. Becoming homesick in her cold tent (owing to a very late spring), Olivia was welcomed into the home of Clare

and Michael's friend and neighbour, Carol Taylor. Their following cosy conversations by the fire – and Carol's boundless enthusiasm and local knowledge – became a fundamental part of Olivia's work on the book. Olivia also met Joan and Charlie Weeks, who helped with everything from where to find a certain model of vintage tractor ("that would be Owen Howill you need to see") to producing a cushion and a tray of tea when she was sitting in the car park drawing the church. Joan, in fact, was the model for Aunty Peggy waving Pippa off on the first page of the story and Owen became the model for Farmer Yelland.

After a week of tracing the Round the Island route, Olivia felt she had everything she needed to begin work on the book back in the studio. On meeting Michael and Clare in Newcastle a few months later, he asked her if she was planning on returning to the village before she finished the book. "I don't think so," she replied. "Why?" "Well," Michael said, "it's just that I'd need to warn the locals…"

In 2012 this remarkable book, three years in the making, was finally published. A simple tale of one girl's childhood, it is also about the magic of the countryside, and how we can unlock this magic with poetry. It is now waiting on shelves across the UK for children to pick it up and carry it on their own adventures, going where their wellies take them.

CLARE AND MICHAEL
MORPURGO

OLIVIA
LOMENECH GILL

Michael Morpurgo OBE began writing stories in the early '70s, in response to the need of the children in his class at the primary school in which he taught in Kent. His first book *It Never Rained*, published by Macmillan, was a collection of short stories about his own family, which he used to read to them and to his class at the end of the school day. He has written 127 books since, and was Children's Laureate from 2003 to 2005.

Clare Morpurgo MBE grew up in Iddesleigh, Devon, although she was born in Paddington in London. Her experience of those early years has informed her life and was largely responsible for her creation of Farms for City Children, which has brought some 100,000 inner-city children to the countryside since 1976.

When she is not counting sheep out of the studio window Olivia creates artworks. Usually about people, but not always. She likes making wooden buildings and, with her husband, built the studio where she works. It creaks when it is windy which, in Northumberland, is most of the time, but while the studio is still standing, she continues to work.

Originally trained in theatre, Olivia has worked as a professional artist for over a decade. As a printmaker Olivia has won several major awards and her work has been exhibited at the Royal Academy, the British and London Art Fairs and Duncan Campbell Fine Art. Though she has always worked with stories, and enjoys working with anyone who tells them, poets, musicians and foreign correspondents, *Where My Wellies Take Me* is her first book project. Olivia continues to practise printmaking and painting, would like to do more bookmaking, and harbours a secret desire to learn to play the hurdy-gurdy.

Farms For
City Children

It is now over thirty-five years since the first group of schoolchildren came to spend a week working as farmers at Nethercott in Devon. Since that time, the charity has gone from strength to strength, adding another two farms to the fold – in Wales and in Gloucestershire – and on the lookout for a fourth, this time further north.

The Farms for City Children formula has changed very little. The approach is hands-on: by participating in the life of the farm, the children learn where their food comes from, the importance of looking after the farm animals and the land, and the value of working together as a team.

If anything, the need for the project has become more apparent and more urgent. Socially and economically, there are no fewer disadvantaged children. But in many ways, the disadvantages run deeper: children have less freedom than they ever did; they are losing the capacity to derive pleasure from actively living in and enjoying the world they inhabit. At the farms, they are away from the passive distractions of the TV and computer; together, they share three home-cooked meals a day and learn how fulfilling a simple enjoyment in life and surroundings can be.

All royalties Michael and Clare receive from Where My Wellies Take Me *will be donated to Farms for City Children.* www.farmsforcitychildren.org

Acknowledgements

The authors and illustrator would like to thank the following people for their help with this book.

Carol Taylor, Joan & Charlie Weeks, Les Curtis, Aldis & Peter Banbury, the Lane family, Owen & Ivy Howill, Jane Feaver, Matt Thomas and The Iddesleigh Friendly Society, Patrick – model for Captain, and truly the most handsome horse in the world, Isobella Turnbull – model for Pippa, Charlie Poulsen & Pauline Burbidge, Katrina Porteous, Anne Fairnington, Mary & Stuart Manley, Judy Smith, Vincent Lomenech and, finally, Philippa Perry.

POETRY INDEX

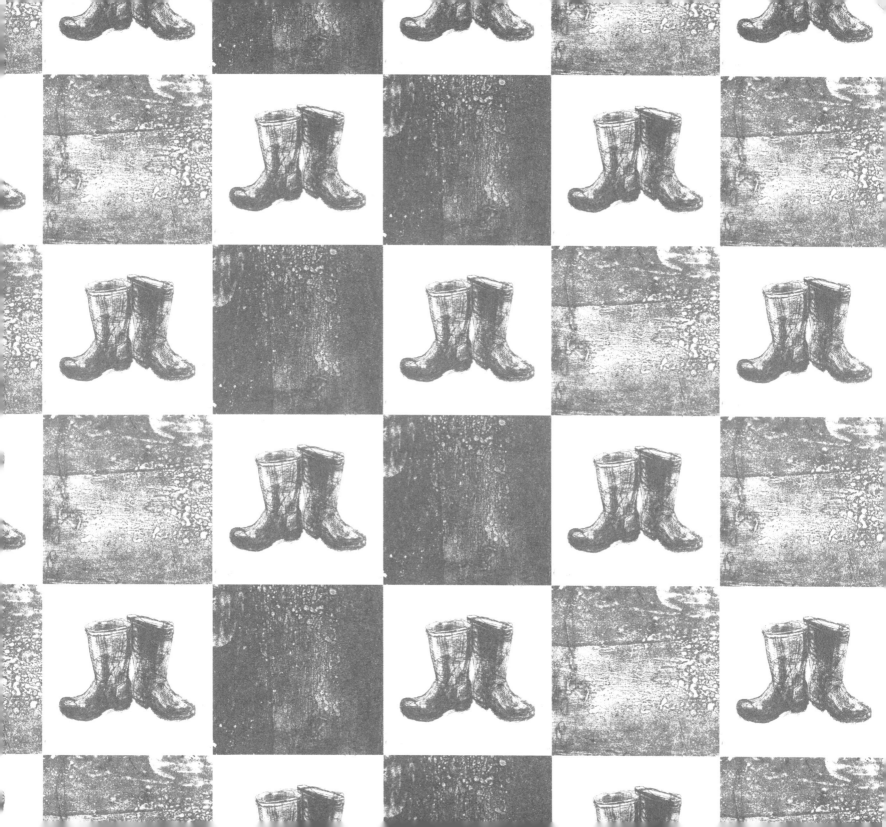

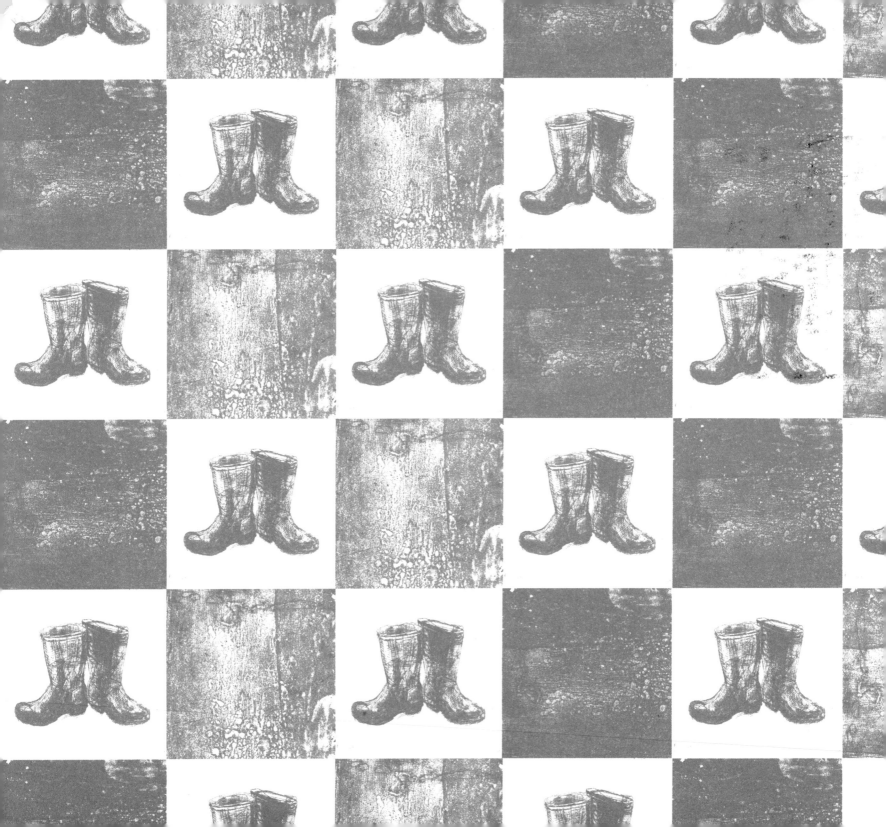